Letters to Bert

A Loving Tribute

By T. H. Waters

Verefor Publishing Company
Minneapolis

Published by
Verefor Publishing Company LLC
Minneapolis, Minnesota

ISBN-13: 978-0-9828931-6-6

Cover design by Robin Ludwig Design Inc.
Supporting Artwork: The Font Diva

Letters to Bert is dedicated to all dogs everywhere who are awaiting the love and care they so justly deserve. I also want to thank the love of my life, my husband Michael, who always believed in me, no matter what.

Books by T. H. Waters also include:
The Rogue Fairy: *Curse of the Queen of Spades*
Ghellow Road: *A literary diary of a young girl's journey*

The Rogue Fairy * Letters to Bert * Ghellow Road
can be ordered from Amazon.com

Please visit T. H. Waters at www.verefor.com

Letters to Bert

A Loving Tribute

Diary Entry 1

Dearest Bert-

I can't believe you are gone. You were getting slow in your old age, sure, but before I knew it, you were no longer on this earth. Maybe I'd been kidding myself for months that nothing was wrong. Maybe I couldn't bear to believe it. I loved you so much. I wasn't ready to let go. You were my Honey Bear, so sweet and loving and gentle. I never even got to say goodbye.

Do you remember the day I brought you home all those years ago? We lived in Minneapolis on Thirteenth Avenue, one block from Minnehaha Creek. Way back then, I volunteered at the Animal Humane Society and had been a dedicated dog walker for about a year by the time our paths crossed. The moment I saw your gentle, loving brown eyes, I knew you had to come home with me. Your eyes. That's one of the things I'll miss most. Those ADORABLE orbs that made you look as though you were part giraffe.

So, there I was at the Animal Humane Society, working my assigned Saturday afternoon shift. It was my turn to walk the shelter dogs on the adoption floor, all twenty-eight of them. The large, rectangular room in which you were all housed until permanent placement was nothing fancy, just your basic gray concrete floors, concrete walls, too, and a few opaque windows; no paint, no frills, but still warm and safe and dry. I began my day at the fenced cage at the front of the room's long, central corridor where a young, excited black lab named Henry was waiting. He jumped on me, then turned around and jumped again. "Down, Boy," I said. "Good, Boy. Good, Boy." Out came a snack. I took him on a short spin outside around the building's perimeter then returned him to his appointed spot and showered him with a few love hugs before leaving. Next up was Coco, an elderly Australian Shepherd charmer. You were third in line. I approached your cage and glanced at your sweet honey-colored face waiting on the other side of the threaded wire that separated us before taking a peek at your stat card: "Collie/Golden Retriever mix – 7 months – 50 pounds - Owner surrender →Dog too large." Too large? What the… ? How could anybody give up on a dog just because it was too large? Dogs *are* large. At least some are. Puppies grow up to become dogs. Some are meant to grow small and some, like Golden Retriever mixes, are meant to grow large! Hello? I'd seen a lot of sad stuff during my tenure as a Humane Society volunteer, more than I care to remember, and was often upset by the callous reasons why some people tossed away a pet. You stood up as soon as I approached and looked at me with mild curiosity. Your eyes said, "Leash? Let's go!"

"Hey cutie," I cooed before opening your cage door. You returned my gaze, alert yet calm, waiting for me to secure the harness. I stood still, anticipating the familiar punch of big paws into my gut like the many I'd already received as a seasoned walker from the dogs who were bored and just plain sick and tired of languishing in their pens. They weren't in the mood to dilly-dally. But you? You were different, eyeing me with your mouth slightly open, thick pink tongue exposed, then glancing from my eyes to the wire cage door and back again. I gave you a few strokes on the head before leading you out into the hallway. You followed my stride, step for step; such a confident boy and regal, too, with no need to bark back at all the jealous hecklers. At the ripe old age of seven months, you already knew your lofty place in the canine chain of command.

That's it. That's all it took. I was hooked from that moment on. After our walk around the building, I returned you to your cage, wrapped my arms around your fluffy, golden neck and gave you a big squeeze before finishing my shift. When it was time for me to clock out, I slowly headed downstairs to the volunteer lockers, lost in my thoughts. You were the only thing on my mind; not my Hubby at home who'd banish me to the Tower of London if I dared bring home another pet; not the husky mix I'd already convinced him to adopt 6 months ago; and not the shelter kitty cat who presently ruled the roost. You were one in a million, and *that* was the only explanation I needed for what I did next. I raced back upstairs to your cage and put a "hold" sign on it, then strode straight to the Adoption Desk to fill out the necessary forms, signing my name on the dotted line. Done. Looking back, that was, by far, the easy part.

Hubby was tinkering in our cramped, urbanish garage when I pulled in beside him. He looked happy to see me at first, that is, right up until the instant he noticed your shaggy face sprouting from between the two front bucket seats. His demeanor changed from pleased to outraged in the span of about a nano second. I can't say I was surprised. I was expecting it, actually. But I was young back in those days and still had plenty of foolish to spend. The way I saw it, you were worth the price of a teensy weensy marital argument that was bound to last merely hours.

"What's that?" asked Hubby, half growling as he pointed in your direction.

I tried to explain, assuring him that you were the best dog on the planet, promising, swearing to the heavens, in fact, that you'd be our last fur-bearing acquisition. "I promise, promise, promise, promise," I pleaded, trying to defuse him.

"You've got to take him back. Monday morning!" snarled my generally easy-go-lucky husband.

It was Saturday afternoon. *Uh oh. This is going to be one hell of a long weekend.*

Turns out, I was correct-o. Hubby and I fought and fought and fought about you for the rest of that day, then straight into Sunday evening.

"He's awesome," I shouted.

"But, we don't *need* another dog."

"You don't understand… I *need* this dog."

"No you don't!"

"Yes I do!"

"No you don't!"

Believe it or not, by the time Sunday night rolled around, I felt defeated.   A line had been drawn in the sand.   I would have to take you back to the shelter the following morning.   I wanted you for my own more than anything but came to the agonizing conclusion that it simply wasn't worth upsetting the state of my union.

I didn't sleep well that night and hauled myself out of bed early Monday morning, my thoughts hazy from lack of sleep.   I was in Million Dollar Man slow motion as I wandered about the house, dressing for my workday and throwing back a quick breakfast of oatmeal.   Hubby kept his distance, quietly observing the crestfallen look that was plastered to my face.

Shortly before I was ready to leave the house, Hubby walked over to me and tenderly placed an arm around my shoulder.   "We can keep him," he said softly.

"What? Really?!"   I was happy, surprised, relieved.   You were going to be mine after all.

♥♥♥

The first night you stayed with us, I hesitantly made the decision to set up your sleeping quarters in our basement; I'd learned earlier from your shelter card information that your previous owners had housed you outside, 24/7, which was another thing that made my blood boil.   It did leave me wondering, though, if you'd been toilet trained, and I didn't want to risk it.   Well, you cried and cried and cried all night long.   Listening to your loud whimpers broke my heart into a million pieces, so the second night I made a blanket bed for you on the floor of our master bedroom, right next to our husky mix, Ernie.   You didn't cry at all, not one peep, and it turned out that you were potty trained after all… much to my relief. All you wanted was no more than what anybody wants, to be hanging with your pack.

Ernie was head-over-heels in love with you on the spot. It was as if he hadn't known how much fun life could really be before you showed up, and was thrilled to have a buddy. I always got the feeling he fancied you more than the other way around, but in time you eventually returned his affection. Each night from then on, the two of you would sleep side by side, nestled into one another.

You had so much energy back then. It's hard to believe it now after watching you slowly disintegrate from the weight of your twelve years on earth. You were often too excited for me to handle. By the time we adopted you, I was still a rookie puppy parent and had a lot to learn about dogs; I needed to understand how to make life good for not only you, but also for me. Co-existence is what they call it. Tricky business. In the very beginning, I didn't walk you everyday like I should have; it was more of a sporadic event whenever the mood happened to hit me. I have to admit… that wasn't my brightest idea. You were such a big puppy, especially for a 7-month-old. It didn't take me long to figure out that you needed to stretch and run and jump and frolic to burn off any excess oomph. During those first walks, I would take you and Ernie along the backside of the creek near our house, that secret place of lanky willows and thick oaks tucked alongside the knee-deep water which only dog lovers and under-aged high school burnouts knew about. I would let you and Ernie off your leashes and man could you two run! Ernie was always faster and you could never catch him. He loved it when you would chase him, and you seemed to enjoy it for years until you turned about nine and figured out that pursuing your brother in big, sweeping circles, literally going nowhere, was kind of a dumb idea after all.

After living together for a few months, I soon learned that we would all be better off if I started increasing the number of your weekly walks. I surprised myself at how much I looked forward to those outings with you; they helped me relax, ponder, enjoy the beauty of nature, and, best of all, laugh at your silly antics. Whenever another dog approached you and

Ernie, your buddy would always, *always* roll over on his back.
Not you. Oh no. You'd stand your ground. You were the
alpha after all, the Lion King, and weren't about to be pushed
around by anyone, no matter how big or small. I admired you
for that.

One marvelous day that first summer, after you'd lived
with us for only a few months, I brought you and Ernie to the
wooded splendor land at the end of our block, just as I always
did after I got home from work. There was a long, grassy hill,
which divided that section of woods, often used for sledding in
the winter but essentially deserted come summertime. The two
of you loved to run down it and sniff, sniff, sniff, then run into
a patch of trees, chasing the frisky squirrels. Unbeknownst to
me, it just so happened that a young couple had decided to
enjoy a romantic picnic on that particular day, right smack dab
in the middle of *our* hill. Well, dummy me had already let you
two off your leashes before I ever had the chance to spy the
pair lounging contentedly on a blanket, their backs facing us.
Mistake doesn't even describe the situation. The instant you
smelled that barbeque, you began running towards the
unsuspecting twosome, chasing treasure, full tilt. Did you
happen to catch the look on that poor guy's face as he
scrambled off his love nest and into the woods? He was clearly
bemused by a 55-pound bundle of Fido barreling towards him
at the speed of light. Not cool to do in front of his little lady,
especially considering that wasn't *her* reaction. I think his
little maneuver may have cost him, if you know what I mean. I
sped after you, struggling to keep my composure. "Bert!
Bert!" I screamed before you finally stopped about ten yards
short of the confused pair. I was so embarrassed. All I could
do was squeak out an apology.

♥♥♥

When you were younger, you loved to chew things. Boy,
did that drive me nuts. You finally outgrew such a terrible
habit, but not before leaving a chomped oriental rug and a

mangled dining room table leg in your wake, among many other expensive and unfortunate targets. For the sake of avoiding more casualties, Hubby and I decided that we had no choice but to keep you and Ernie kenneled while we were away. Oh, how you hated your kennel! We tried to be thoughtful and make it as much of a *home away from home* as we could, lining your cage with blankets for you to lie on, but you'd chew holes in them to no avail. I went half-crazy with worry. You got us back, though. Yep. We tried to secure your kennel door with at least one latch, but Houdini Pup somehow always figured out how to escape, even though it never mattered *how many* latches we put on. Two, three, four? It was an incredible sleight of hand. We could never figure out how the heck you managed to be waiting by the back door every time we arrived home after work. But the cycle remained unbroken; morning after morning we'd load you into your crate before leaving, thinking "this time…" and evening after evening we'd come home to find you roaming.

After we'd been living in our house for a while, we thought it best to build a fence around our backyard so that you and Ernie could safely romp. Okay, so maybe it was 100% my idea. Hubby wasn't all that keen about it since he was the one who would have to build it! Well, you know how I've always been… how shall I say this… a worrywart; worry about this and worry about that. I gave Hubby a gentle nudge, asking if he would build the highest fence possible so that you and Ernie wouldn't be able to vault off the winter snow banks into freedom. "You're crazy," said Hubby flatly. Well I guess I probably was, but I just couldn't take a chance and have you end up at the dog pound or, worse yet, hit by a car. So, I asked Hubby to install a six-foot privacy fence. Yes, I was sure six feet would do nicely. "Six feet?!" he asked, clearly skeptical. He didn't think that was a very good idea but eventually agreed after a lot of nagging and plenty of chocolate chip cookie bribes and pie, lots and lots of pie. In hindsight, it really was a ridiculous idea. Hubby had been right after all. By the time he was finished with the project, we had this enormous wooden plank fence completely surrounding our tiny city lot. It was beyond claustrophobic. I could never see anything on either side of our yard whenever I'd walk from the garage to the house. I'm certain we convinced the neighbors that we had something to hide. Mary Jane horticulturists, perhaps? Nudists, maybe? Whatever. REALLY DUMB IDEA.

One day when we were on a walk, you and Ernie kept pulling me and pulling me, even more than usual. You were strong, too, and I'm not exactly a burly woman. I thought both arms were going to spring from my sockets. Finally, I couldn't take it anymore. I was so flustered and upset by the time we got home that I told you I was never going to take you on a walk again. Ever. That little episode turned out to be the springboard for my next brilliant idea... to enroll you and Ernie in obedience class. Remember what a fiasco that was? Oh, brother. We went to class once a week at the local high school gym, for what *should have* been eight full weeks. At first I thought it was going to be fun. High hopes had I. And I was absolutely certain that after we'd completed training, you'd become a perfect dog who would never dream of pulling on the leash when we walked. The best damn dog on the planet, who just happened to be mine, would listen attentively to my every command. Um. Yeah, that's the thinking of someone who has never raised a dog before. Every Wednesday night, Hubby and I would religiously pack you and Ernie into our car and off we'd go to class. There were lots of other dogs there, maybe twenty, big, small, shaggy, skinny, fat, but none were as cool as you. Not even close. Hubby decided he wanted to be in charge of Ernie, so that made me in charge of you, by default. As the strict obedience class instructor barked orders at us, you and I would take a crack at each exercise. Or, at least *try* to take a crack at each exercise. You never learned a damn thing. It drove me bananas. You were constantly staring at Ernie, who just so happened to always be on the opposite side of the room, and you never heard a word I said. I'd get so mad at you, "Bert! Bert! Pay attention. You have to listen to me!" Ha! Fat chance. You didn't want anything to do with the whole ridiculous escapade. You know that cartoon where a man is talking to his dog in complex sentences but all the dog hears is "blah, blah, blah?" Yeah well, it was exactly like that. I think you were secretly giving Ernie eye signals to help you exit, stage left. One night, on the second to the final class, I simply lost it. I was trying to give you a command for the umpteenth time, and that's when you decided that you'd had enough of my bossiness. You laid on the floor and rolled onto your back. Yep. While all the other doggies were minding their guardians, you were wriggling around on your back. Sure, it's funny *now,* but at the time I was seething. My frustration level skyrocketed. I sat down crossed-legged next to you on the gym floor and practically burst into tears, right then and there. I couldn't take it anymore. I caught Hubby's eye and motioned "Let's Go!" At least *he* was willing to obey me. We left immediately and never returned. From that moment on, you were an official dog school drop out.

Time abated my frustration after a few weeks had passed, and I made the bold decision to train you myself, far away from all the noise and distraction of other dogs. From then on, it was going to be just me, you and a pocketful of snacks. And, by God, it worked. Little by little, you were actually becoming an obedient dog. We started going on more walks, and I'd practice commands every chance I got. "Heel, Bert. Good boy. Sit, Bert. So good. Stay, Bert. Here's a Snausage, Honey." Eventually, and much to my astonishment, you actually did become the best damn dog on the planet, bar none. I was so proud of you! I would always beam whenever passers-by would admire you and tell me how wonderful you were. "I know," I'd ooze. You had become my sweet, obedient Honey Bear, and, in the process, I learned more than you did.

♥♥♥

Like I said, both you and Ernie were so full of energy when you were young. I couldn't help but strategize on creative ways to discharge it. Sometimes my ideas paid off and sometimes they didn't. Way back then, Hubby and I had recently discovered a new phenomenon known as Rollerblades. I can't recall who thought of it, but one of us got the ingenious idea of taking you and Ernie along whenever we'd skate around Lake Nokomis on the weekends. You two absolutely loved this strange new game and never seemed to tire, even when we'd run you for three miles at a pretty good pace. We all enthusiastically embraced our new pastime until one day things went wrong, very, very wrong. It was on a bright and sunny Saturday morning in the middle of summer, the type of day that makes you feel invincible. I leashed up Ernie while Hubby took care of you. I'm not the earliest of birds, so we got a late start that morning. The lake was pretty crowded by the time we skated onto the scene; half-naked teenagers crowded the sandy beach, mothers pushed baby strollers along the tarred walking path, bikes zoomed around the lake's rim in their own designated lane. The weather couldn't have been more beautiful, more perfect. So, there we were, skating around the lake in the bike lane without a care, having a splendid time when… BAM! Disaster struck. A middle-aged woman was peddling her three-speed towards us from the opposite direction, her small, leashed dog running alongside. Just as she and Hubby intersected, that white fluff ball of hers decided to pick a fight and lunged at you, barking his nasty, little head off. Well, you were never one to take shit off *n-o-b-o-d-y*, so you snapped right back, and then moved in closer to take a chomp out of his head. In that precise moment you accidentally merged into the path of The Rollerblading Husband who promptly toppled over your back. He instinctively put his hands in front of him to break the fall, and that's when we both heard the terrible noise. "Snap!" The course of history had been changed forever; Hubby cleared you but had broken both elbow joints, just like that. I freaked out and ran over to help. He gritted his teeth and winced, "I think I just broke my arms."

That's when my heart plunged into my stomach. I quickly
scanned his limp limbs, searching for a hopeful sign. There
weren't any protruding bones, yet he couldn't move. Not at all.
I panicked at first, then regained composure enough to tie you
and Ernie to the nearest tree. I helped Hubby scoot off the bike
path and onto the grass next to you, then bladed home as fast as
I could to retrieve our car. When I returned twenty minutes
later, I quickly installed everyone in the sedan, dogs in the back
seat and Hubby in the front passenger seat, and then hightailed
it to the emergency room. Yep, it turned out that Hubby had
been right, he had indeed broken both of his elbows. My poor
guy! So, for an entire week he was outfitted in not one but *two*
casts and couldn't do anything for himself. And I mean
ANYTHING. I felt so badly for him. He wasn't able to work,
prepare meals, or eat by himself. He couldn't even hold a beer
bottle. And he sure as hell couldn't use the facilities by
himself, if you know what I mean. Yep. The Wife had to tend
to a few unpleasant tasks. As for that dumb-dumb woman and
her rogue dog, we never did see them again. Hubby eventually
fully recovered and got back into his normal routine, including
the use of his beer holding hand. We never took you two
rollerblading again.

♥♥♥

I love big dogs, absolutely adore them to pieces, and when
you came home with me all those years ago, I wished and
wished you'd grow to weigh at least one hundred pounds.
Well, I got my wish. By the time you turned two years old you
did indeed weigh almost exactly one hundred pounds! There
was a downside to your largeness, most definitely, but there
were also tangible benefits, like how safe and at ease I felt
whenever you were near. It was like living with a professional
linebacker who would kick anybody's butt should they dare
mess with me. But… sometime during that last year of your
life, I knew you were no longer able to protect me. I could
sense your strength fading away; I could sense your

vulnerability. I buried that forewarning deep within because I simply couldn't handle the thought of you becoming an old dog, a dog that would leave me one day, and so quickly at that.

Do you remember when Hubby and I brought the kitties home for the first time? To be honest, I can't recall your reaction as much as I can remember theirs. It was a snowy Saturday in the middle of a typical Minnesota December when Hubby and I brought two new kitties home from the local Humane Society. Yep, the same one where I volunteer. Our elder kitty had recently passed and I was missing her. Even though we already had you two dogs, I was convinced we needed to increase the size of our colony. No need to remind me about that promise to Hubby, or that I have what's known as Noah's Ark syndrome. I was lucky that Hubby would usually go along with whatever wild idea du jour I happened to be obsessing over… most of the time anyway, and I was in the middle of obsessing over kitty cats. So, frisky gray Bono and mellow black Edge came to live with us in our small, humble Tudor on Thirteenth Avenue. As soon as we arrived home with our fur-bearing bundles, we guided you and Ernie into the living room to meet your new roomies, who were presently secured in their carriers. Mistake. BIG mistake. The very moment we released the kitties, they bolted for cover. And I'm talkin' b-o-l-t-e-d. They flashed past us so fast and furiously that we could barely figure out where they'd hidden. Those poor little guys were absolutely petrified. Not you and Ernie, though. Forget about it. You were both so nonchalant and far more curious about what those two black and gray extraterrestrials *were* more than anything. After a few hours had passed, the kitties gathered enough courage to come out from their hiding place beneath the couch and quickly learned that you and Ernie were friends, not foes. In time, they eventually grew to love you. Remember how Bono would rub against you all the time? He'd stand up on his hind legs and push his face into your furry chest. You, on the other hand, weren't interested in such odd intimacy. Sure, you liked him fine enough, but you just weren't into felines. They couldn't accompany you on walks, for one thing, or figure out how to open the treat drawer. Even still, you'd allow Bono to worship you but would soon become bored and casually stroll away. He'd trail behind for a few minutes before zooming off in search of some other amusement. The Edge, on the other hand, had only three things on his mind #1 food #2 food #3 food and wasn't the slightest bit interested in befriending you because A) you weren't food and B) you didn't know how to get him any. Needless to say, the two of you got along splendidly.

♥♥♥

When you were still young, I decided to take you running with me, just the two of us. I'd already tried it with Ernie. He was inherently intuitive and glided by my side with ease, always seeming to know when to turn right and when to turn left. We made a great team. I expected you to be the same way. Nope. You weren't, not in the least, and my experiment turned out to be a disaster. Every time I'd try to move in a forward motion, your herding instincts would kick in, and you'd begin pushing me to one side of the trail or the other. You'd bark and jump at me before plowing your big hulk right in front of my path. It was adorable and annoying as hell all at the same time. Okay, okay, we never made much progress, and I'd always end up frustrated. I wanted to give you some much-needed exercise, but you simply weren't the dog for the job. After all, you were an obedience school drop out. In the end, I took you out only a few more times before hanging up your running shoes for a while. It was time to try something different.

♥♥♥

Diary Entry 2

Dearest Bert,

It's been almost three weeks now since you've passed. I'm still missing you and cry almost every night. Sometimes a lot, and other times just a little. I went to a pet loss therapy group last night and reluctantly shared my grief with others who feel the same. Some days I feel like I'm doing pretty good, considering the circumstances, but then something will trigger my memories of you, and I'll break down again.

♥♥♥

Our little family had resided at the Thirteenth Avenue house for only a few years before I started getting restless in my corporate job and craved a change. After many gut-wrenching conversations with Hubby, we finally decided upon a new direction. We'd be moving into a "fixer-upper" and renovating it. Hey, why not? It seemed like a pretty good idea at the time. Housing prices were trending upward in the early 90's, and Hubby and I were both pretty handy around the house; I was a good painter, he was a good carpenter and we both knew our way around tile and grout. Maybe we'd never had any formal training, but how hard could it really be? So says the voice of a twenty-something. After a short search with our realtor, we found the perfectly suited house in Linden Hills, one of the best neighborhoods in the city limits. It was a shabby, traditional two-story with great potential. The perfect ticket. The very week we closed on our brand new home, I chucked my day job, Hubby took a deep breath and an even deeper shot of whiskey (totally not kidding), and we began our new life as pseudo-professional home remodelers.

♥♥♥

I became more and more attached as you began to grow up. I'd never had a dog before you and Ernie came along. so I guess I never realized just how strong our bond would become. During the previous chapter in our lives when Hubby and I were beating our brains out daily in the business world, we had no choice but to leave you two home alone. Now, our newfound lifestyle afforded a welcomed reprieve, one that offered some much needed independence for us all. I could get up whenever I wanted, take a shower (or not) whenever I wanted. There were no deadlines to meet, and nobody was around to hover over my shoulder, barking unreasonable demands. Ahhh, sweet freedom.

I relished my new life and was determined to take full advantage of it. Who knew how long it would last? Each morning welcomed a new expedition and we'd celebrate. first thing, with a leisurely walk. We did oodles of exploration, sniffing out the new neighborhood gems. Sometimes we'd run into other dogs along the way, and you'd always want to say 'Howdy." One of your favorites was an adorable golden retriever named Lucky. His guardian took him for a walk just about everyday and was as devoted to Lucky as that little sweetie was to him. One summer morning when we were out meandering through the neighborhoods, I spied a handsome old dog who was walking towards us with a middle-aged woman, he was on one side of the street while we were on the other. A festive paper party hat was tied to the top of his head, and he was moving quite slowly. As we neared, his guardian beamed at me and shouted, "He's celebrating his fourteenth birthday!" I smiled and roared my congratulations. "I hope mine make it that far!" I will never forget looking at the two of you that morning and hoping with all my might that I'd never have to witness your vitality fade in the same way it had with that handsome 14-year-old. At the time, it seemed impossible. For so many years your spunk was larger than the state of Texas; you'd wake up eons before I ever did and couldn't wait for me to get out of bed. If you ever sensed I was stirring, even just a little, you'd bound over to my side of the bed and push your wet nose into my cheek. That was your sweet way of say, "Get up now 'cuz it's time to romp!" And whenever we'd walk, you'd hold your head so high, a beautiful smile spread across your face. Oh, how I loved that smile.

♥♥♥

Diary Entry 3

Dearest Bert,

Today is Sunday morning. I walked over to the Holiday gas station with Ernie. On our way home, we took an unusual route and happened upon a threesome who were kneeling beside a black dog, one of them gently securing it by the collar so that it wouldn't bound away. As we approached, they asked if the dog was mine and explained that they'd found it running loose. I stopped to chat with them while they waited for the dog's rightful guardian to appear and claim him. While the minutes passed, I carefully observed the black dog. He didn't look much like you, yet he had that same undeniable gentle presence. I walked over to him and was slow to gingerly stroke his fluffy fur. When I looked into his eyes I saw none other than yours staring back at me; those same brown eyes of deep devotion. Otis softly licked my hand, and my heart let in a little light of hope. Not long afterwards, his guardian pulled up, and I sadly watched him ride away. The woman who'd initially found him looked at me and teased, "Only a few more minutes and you'd have had yourself a brand new dog!" Yes, I would have loved that. I would have loved Otis to fill up my house and heart, but I'm not ready yet and am still shell-shocked from what happened to you. I need plenty more time to heal.

♥♥♥

As I mentioned earlier, I was becoming more and more attached to you as time went on and was trying to weave you and Ernie into my daily life. I took the two of you with me whenever I could, wherever I could. Hubby and I would occasionally bring you two along to breakfast at the Gingerbread Café. Do you remember that cute little joint in Linden Hills right next to the barbershop? Every summer the Gingerbread Café would place a few token tables in front of their establishment. It wasn't much of a hot spot, an old-timer that had been around for years, languishing in its old ways of doing business by refusing to give in to the trendy wave of all those so-called fancy pants who were keen on taking over. It wasn't nearly half as adorable as its name would imply, especially when you factor in the cramped indoor seating and massive plumes of cigarette smoke. But it was close to our house, maybe eight blocks away, really just a hop, skip and a jump. We'd sit down at one of the outside tables and tie you two boys to the table legs. You were well-behaved, usually lying on the pavement beside us and wagging your tails while inhaling all those heavenly breakfast smells that can only be churned out from a bona fide greasy spoon, patiently waiting for your well-deserved treat at the end of the meal. Much to our chagrin, we always ended up with the same waitress, an older woman with short gray hair who'd been in the biz since she was ten years old, *I swear*. She despised our company so much that she had no qualms what-so-ever about making her annoyance perfectly clear; exaggerated exhaustion was commonplace each time she stepped around you while taking our order or delivering the goodies. No matter. We always gave her an extra tip for her troubles.

I often enjoyed frequenting the local grocery store in our neighborhood, which sat just around the corner from the Gingerbread Cafe. Sometimes I'd drive there with the two of you in the back seat, while other times we'd walk. You and I strolled over there one afternoon that first summer, just the two of us, and I needed a place to tie you while I ran inside. A few utilitarian metal tables and chairs had been set up along the sidewalk in front for the patrons to use, seeming like an ideal place to park you for a few minutes. After securing you, I scurried inside, scanned my shopping list, collected my merchandise in record time and then out the door I went. As I was exiting the store, I heard a loud banging noise echoing off the cement. *Uh oh*, I thought. *What just happened?* I rushed outside to retrieve you and froze in my tracks, mouth agape, as you sped down the sidewalk in the opposite direction, heading straight for the nearest intersection. Something must have spooked you while I was in the store, causing you to charge off. And when that big-ass unidentified flying object started chasing you from behind, it prompted you to gallop even faster. What a sight, to say the least. I squinted my eyes while my mind churned slowly, trying to process what was happening before finally shifting into high gear. I panicked and shouted for you to stop. "Bert! Stop! Stop! Wait! What are you doing?!" I doubt you could have heard me over the angry clanging of that stupid table. Lucky for me, and for you too, a kind soul was waiting to cross the street near that particular corner and managed to intercept you before you harmed yourself. Holy banana peels, was I relieved. I wanted to smooch that guy for saving you. That's when I got the shivers just thinking about the harm you could have done to yourself had you run into the street. And I don't even want to imagine what could have happened to a small child in your path. Thankfully, nothing tragic happened and that whole escapade ended up being nothing more than a funny memory.

Back when we all lived in the Abbott house, I would take you and Ernie for long, leisurely walks, usually never less than a few miles or so. Although we no longer resided near Minnehaha Creek and its adjacent verdant acres thick with willows and pines, we still had access to plenty of lush, natural spaces and block upon block of comely, well-kept homes. I fancied mixing things up a bit and was continually creating new routes through our neighborhoods. On one of our favorites, we'd make our way from our two-story stucco in the southwest corner of Minneapolis and head west to Edina, the

nearest neighboring city. France Avenue is the clear-cut line
that precisely divides those who are wealthy from those who
live humbly, and I thoroughly enjoyed taking you along with
me to tour those upper-crust neighborhoods, often referring to
them as Candyland, one of my favorite childhood games. The
fortunate residents of Candyland lived in big, beautiful houses
and drove big, beautiful cars, earning mountains of money to
boot. Memberships to exclusive country clubs were about as
common as the hired help, and appointed days named in their
honor by the state's governor were boringly expected. House
after house was divine brick and stucco perfection, so much so
that the entire neighborhood landed on the National Register of
Historic Places. Defiantly undaunted by such affluence, our
disheveled pack of three would wind our way through the elite
streets; you two sniffing for bear while I admired the flawless
architecture. We happened upon a quaint park on one
particular day, right smack dab in the middle of the Candyland
oasis. No one was around, the kids were all in school. I
released you two hounds and off you went, sprinting this way
and that, and then dashing back the instant I called your names.
That wonderful, little park turned out to be one of my favorite
spots, and yours, too. We were sure to visit often.

♥♥♥

In all the years that you and I have been together, there
was only one tragic event in your life, but boy, was it a doozie.
It was when Hubby and I were working full-time. We were
leery of our furry four-footed troublemakers while we were
away, so we crated you and Ernie each morning before we left
the house. Constantly in a hurry to get off to work, we never
gave much thought to consequence, grabbing the nearest toys
at hand and throwing them into your crate, hoping they would
occupy and distract you for a few hours. Although I'd recently
resigned from my accounting job, they'd asked me to stay on
until a replacement could be found. Translation... you and
Ernie would have to continue resting in your crates each day

until Hubby and I returned home. One morning we made the near-fatal mistake of including a Frisbee with your toy collection. When I returned home that afternoon, I took you and Ernie outside for your usual bathroom break. I could tell immediately that something was wrong. You didn't greet me with your same big floppy smile, that "I'm so happy to see you" look. Instead, you were walking far slower than your two-and-a-half years and didn't even try to relieve yourself once outside. After I led you back inside, you were overcome by the dry heaves. A warning whistle started to blow inside my head. When I offered you some kibble, you refused to eat. Not eat kibble? What? That's when I was sure that something was *definitely* wrong. I was scared now. I phoned Hubby at work, and he raced home. As soon as he arrived, we packed you into the car and gassed it for the local vet. After we bolted through the entrance, the veterinarian staff informed us that no one was available to assist us because they were all attending their annual state conference. And by the way, every vet from every other clinic was doing the same thing. What? We couldn't believe our terrible luck. How could every damn vet in the entire city be out of commission? Well, we had no choice but to take you back home and monitor you. My insides were twisting tighter and tighter as we helplessly watched you become sicker and sicker by the minute, so we packed you back into the car and raced you to the emergency vet where they looked you over and ran a few tests. The vet on call wasn't able to diagnose the problem, so it was back to square one. Monitor, monitor, monitor is what we did for the next several hours back at home. We were so scared and nervous that I doubt we even bothered to eat anything. Your condition wasn't changing so we had no choice but to race you back to the emergency vet. After running more tests and performing x-rays, she was finally able to tell us what was wrong.... you'd chewed a chunk of the plastic Frisbee and it had severed several inches of your intestine. Whoa... come again??? How could I have been so stupid to give you a Frisbee? Ridiculously stupid? Yes! But there was nothing I could do

about it at that moment. I was a wreck. The vet advised us to
send you into surgery, *stat*. She stated frankly that it would be
touch and go – there was a chance you wouldn't make it
through. We stayed at the clinic until you'd recovered from the
anesthesia, then Hubby and I took you back home in silence,
our hearts as heavy as lead. You were so weak; the sight of
your now listless body made me ill to the bone. Hubby and I
carried your 100-pound frame through the front door and
gently laid you on our couch. We knew you'd be too feeble to
climb the stairs to the master bedroom, so we rounded up an
old mattress from the basement and parked it on our living
room floor. That would be your very own bed for the next
several weeks. Hubby and I took turns sleeping on the couch
beside you each night. We hand-prepared all of your food
according to the vet's directions and offered it to you, but you
wouldn't eat any. We were petrified. You'd always loved
food more than just about anything. Things were not looking
good. The work week rolled around again and Monday a.m.
was upon us with a vengeance. We were afraid to leave you
alone while we went to our jobs, so we made arrangements
with our local vet to care for you from eight o'clock in the
morning until five o'clock each night. As the days passed, you
were ever so s-l-o-w-l-y becoming stronger. Finally, *finally*
you were eating once more, and I will never forget when that
feisty spark flooded back into your eyes. I'd drop you off at
the vet each morning of that last week and all the female
technicians would purr, "Hi, Handsome!" whenever you'd
saunter into their waiting room. They'd rave, "What a great
dog!" Well, of course. You were the best damn dog on the
planet. Miraculously, you bounced back from your near-death
experience after only a few weeks and were back to your
adorable, happy self. All was right with the world once more.

♥♥♥

Diary Entry 4

Dearest Bert,

I went to the state fair last Friday with Hubby and had the time of my life. I think I was so tired of being sad. As daylight was transforming to dusk, we hopped the Skyride, which is basically nothing more than a pimped out ski lift, and cruised over to the opposite side of the fairgrounds. As we were approaching our drop-off site, I spied a building with the word "Purina" emblazoned on the side and knew that I had to go there. Although all the lights were still on when we entered, it was clear that most of the day's dog show participants and their owners had skedaddled, while only a handful of stragglers remained to pack up their belongings. We wandered about for a few minutes, exploring, and that's when I noticed that a few of the woofers had not yet gone home. I moved in closer because you know how I can't resist a woofer! There were three gorgeous Collie/Golden mixes (just like you!) sitting in one of the booths. One in particular had me at "Hello," and I couldn't take my eyes off him. He'd perched himself on a small table and was calmly surveying his territory, patiently waiting to leave. He was even breathing through his mouth in that same funny way you always had. Do you remember? Your mouth would open just slightly, and as the air passed across your tongue it would push out your cheeks like a goldfish does as it passes water through its gills or like a man smoking a cigar. Puff, puff, puff. I loved it when you'd breathe like that. It was so comical and always brought a smile to my face. I wanted to take that dog home right then and there, but even more than that I wanted you back. I still go for walks each morning and bring your leash. I keep it in my pocket and hold on tightly. I think of you as I'm breezing along, shedding my morning tears to get them out before facing the world again. Thoughts of you happily running through the grass cross my mind like a home movie that keeps rewinding over and over. I hope that each and everyday you were on this planet you felt my immense love for you, despite my preoccupation with life, with work, with responsibilities. I wish you could come back to me so that I could feel whole once more.

♥♥♥

I suppose I should get back to happy times…

You became even more loyal than ever after that horrible Frisbee incident, I'm talkin' fiercely loyal. Up to that point, you and I had built a strong bond, to be sure, but something in you changed after you'd fully recovered from your near-death experience. It was almost as if you felt a need to repay Hubby and me for giving you a second chance at life.

Not long after that dreadful experience, Hubby and I were working on yet another house remodeling project and had opened a window on the landing leading up to the second floor so that our house could breathe. Well, that window had no screen, of course, and we should have known better, BUT… you know how that goes. Back then, my little black fur-ball kitty cat, Edge, was always looking for ways to escape. Who knows why? He was such a piglet and a lover of comfort. How could he have possibly envisioned a better life than the one he'd currently been leading? But somehow he did and decided that he was going to make yet another break for freedom through no other passage than that damn open window. I was there and saw him with my own two freaked-out eyes when he leapt up onto the ledge and nonchalantly gazed down at the concrete below him. I could just see his itchy little wheels turning as he contemplated whether or not it was worth the jump. Well, apparently he decided that it was and off he plunged, the whole 10 feet! Like I said, where in the hell did he think he was going? Of course I went manic as soon as I saw the last of his black furry tail disappear from sight. I immediately bolted for the front door and scanned the

yard for any sign of the streaking blob. As soon as I spotted
the little fella, I took off after him. Before I knew it, that damn
Schnauzer dog from across the street was in the mix. He must
have been hanging out in his yard, looking for action, and
wasn't able to resist a good chase. My poor, little Edge was
the bait! Holy crap!! So, here was this damn dog chasing my
kitty. Who knows why? And then there was me, running
behind the two of them. So, picture this... a chubby black cat
being chased by a Miniature Schnauzer being chased by a
hysterical cat mama. Probably a humorous sight to the casual
observer, but not so for me. I was scared as hell. I mean, that
dog was acting like it wanted to chew my little Edgeward to
shreds. So, the three of us were running across the front lawns
on our block with no resolution in sight, not a good one,
anyway. Before I knew it, you went barreling past me
(emerging from a phone booth in our house, no doubt!). After
a few more gallops, you'd reached that bratty little dog and
took a hefty chomp out of his backside. Yep, that's right. My
little superhero gave him the nip-nip what for! All I could hear
after that was "Yip! Yip! Yip! Yip!" as he ran his sorry ass
back home as fast as he could. I was finally able to scoop up
poor Edge and place him back into our house, safe and
unscathed. THEN I SHUT THE WINDOW. This is one of my
most favorite memories of you. You saved Edge from harm
and, quite possibly, you saved his very life. It was a truly
remarkable act. I have no earthly idea how you managed to
escape our house and come to the rescue because you were still
inside the moment Edge jumped out the window. You must
have heard all the commotion and pushed the screen door with
your long nose so that you could come to our aid. It was times
like that when I knew you were truly special, such a gift to me.

♥♥♥

Diary Entry 5

Dearest Bert,

*   I didn't sleep much last night. I was feeling so much sorrow and cried until about midnight. When I finally did get to sleep, it was the restless kind. The alarm started blaring at 5:30 the next morning, and I begrudgingly slumped out of bed. I'm worn out today. After work, I walked home with a guy who rides my bus. He asked about you because he would always see us walking together around the neighborhood. I glumly told him that you'd passed away unexpectedly five weeks ago while I was at work. He told me that the same thing had happened to his family dog when he was a boy. They suspected the cause was heartworm but were never able to confirm their suspicions because they didn't have enough money for the vet bill. When I heard that, I was so thankful that I'd always been able to pay for your care; your annual check-ups, your stitches after you cut your eyebrow, your emergency surgery bills, your hip dysplasia medication, and that visit we made to the vet six months ago when they checked the mysterious lump on your belly. At that time, the vet said it was only fatty tissue and I had nothing to worry about. After all, most old dogs get mysterious lumps and bumps as they age; it comes with the territory, but now I wonder if it was more than that. Was it cancer? I guess I'll never know. When my bus buddy and I parted ways last night, he said he knew how hard it was to lose a pet and told me that every day gets better and the worst is behind me. He didn't know that you were never my pet. He didn't know that you were one of the best friends I'd ever had in my whole life.*

♥♥♥

    Hubby's parents moved back from the east coast to their
home state of Minnesota during the time when the six of us
were living in the Abbott house. My father-in-law had been
laid off from his executive position at an electronics firm, and
they wanted to live closer to family. The Outlaws owned some
gorgeous lakeshore property near the Brainerd Lakes area in
central Minnesota and decided to build a small log cabin on
their site while Hubby's father continued searching for a decent
job. His mother had kept some furnishings from their previous
home and was using them to create a charming place for the
two of them. The summers at the lake house were picture-
perfect, as anyone who has ever lived in Minnesota knows.
Hubby and I would pack up you and Ernie a handful of times
each cabin season and head up to the beautiful lakes area.
Those are wonderful memories for so many reasons. Back
then, you were still young and full of excitement, but you hated
being in the car because it made your tummy upset. Luckily,
you never threw up *inside* our car, except for that one time
when I fed you a banana right before we left, but that was my
fault. Aside from that, you were able to endure the three-hour
drive and loved being at the cabin as much as we did. We'd all
hang out and relax on the little private sand beach or swim in
the cool lake water, except for Mr. Ernie, who was always too
chicken to swim. Hubby would patiently carry him into the
water with the hope that he'd eventually learn to like it, but
Ernie would turn right back around just as soon as he could and
paddle to shore, lickety-split, enormous, terror-filled eyes wide
open. But with you it was different. Hubby would slowly
wade into the water until it reached the middle of his chest
while you stood rigidly still, cautiously eyeing him from the
sandy shoreline. All Hubby would have to do to entice you
was call your name, "Bert! C'mon, boy. C'mon," and you'd
bravely submerge your big shaggy bulk into the cool depths
and dutifully paddle over to him. As soon as you got close
enough, he'd plunge both his arms into the water and secure
them beneath your belly so that you wouldn't tire, then gently
hold you buoyant for a few minutes before leading you back to

shore where you'd shake and shake and shake…. and SHAKE all the water from your coat. All refreshed, you'd search out Ernie, who was well out of arms reach and *uncatchable*, then chase him around the woods for a while. You and Ernie did so much running in those woods. I'd let the two of you scamper off to wherever you pleased then call your names every once in a while until you'd beat feet towards the sound of my voice. You'd look up at me with an expression that asked, "What's up?" I'd tell you that I just wanted to make sure you were all right and then off you'd go, that is until you heard the sound of my voice calling you back again. Sometimes I'd walk in the woods with you; sometimes other neighbor dogs would come calling and you'd horse around with them for awhile; sometimes you'd sit near us when we roasted marshmallows by the evening bonfire; sometimes you'd opt to just lay beneath the shade of a big, old birch tree in the middle of the afternoon, all wet and happy. No matter what, each and every night you and Ernie would always, always, always sleep near my bed. Life was good…

Hubby and I looked forward to weekend visits with the Outlaws at the cabin. After all, that was, by far, the optimal time to tag along with Mother Outlaw when she went shopping at the nearby antique and gift stores. Before we'd get into her car, she'd suggest that we leave you and Ernie outside until we returned. I knew that we'd be gone no less than two hours and I'd think, "Woman. Are you out of your mind?" What came out of my mouth instead was a sheepish, "Well. I'd feel so much better if they stayed inside the cabin." Mother Outlaw felt it was ridiculous to keep dogs indoors on such a beautiful summer day, but in the end I always got my way. She'd reluctantly call the neighbor girl to come over and baby-sit the two of you. Yep. That's right. I had no shame in hiring a babysitter for four dollars an hour to take care of you while I went antiquing. That money spent was well worth it. I would've rather lost a little money than dealt with the loss of you.

♥♥♥

Diary Entry 6

Dearest Bert,

It's been seven weeks since you left me. I still miss you so much. Luckily, time has been good to me. I feel okay during most of my waking hours and am able to go about my life, but I still break down occasionally and tears begin to fall at the thought of my tremendous loss. I went for a run last night. It was a beautiful autumn evening, and I longed to have you by my side amidst the depth of cool air. As I ran, you drifted into my mind, and I swear I could feel you galloping beside me, just as you used to do when you were younger. I headed past Lynnhurst Park, a favorite haunt where you and Ernie used to play. There were lots of kids running around, playing soccer beneath the glow of the evening stadium lights while their parents watched on, attentively perched in their folding chairs. The faint sound of an ice cream truck floated in the distance. Tears filled my eyes as I let the present day's events be replaced by those of the past. The children faded away right before me, and I could picture an empty field with Ernie running like the wind and you in tow, pumping so hard to keep up with him yet never able, just like it had been for all those years when the two of you ran together. It never really bothered you at the time, though. Your motto had always been, "The joy is in the journey not in the destination." You found beauty in the chase, the outdoors, the sunshine, the fresh grass. As I ran, this image of you stuck in my mind and tears raced down my face and bounced off my cheeks in tandem with each beat of my footsteps against the pavement. I think of you every day, every single day, and I miss you beyond words. Ernie is still here with me. Whenever I'm in the kitchen, he'll lay on the floor nearby, just like you used to do. I wish that I could hug you again just one last time and tell you how much I love you.

♥♥♥

Hubby and I would often take road trips to places that
didn't allow woofers. Luckily for us, The Outlaws would
watch over you and Ernie at their cabin while we escaped from
the daily grind for a few days. I hated to leave you, of course,
but the cabin was such a magical place, and I felt assured that
you'd be well taken care of. Plus, I knew how much you loved
it there. I mean, it was such a cushy life at the lake – it may as
well have been a doggie spa! I will never forget how you acted
whenever Hubby and I dropped you off, and then prepared to
leave without you in our back seat. We'd arrive at the cabin
with you and Ernie, pull into the driveway, park, and then pop
inside for a short visit while you two bounded through the thick
woods. When it was time to be on our way, we'd head toward
our car, and there you'd be, right by our side. Ernie was never
anywhere in sight. He was far more interested in chasing
bunny rabbits then giving us a proper send off. But not you.
You hated to see us leave and wouldn't budge. I'd always hug
and kiss you good-bye, promising we'd return in just a few
short days. I'd get into the car while you stood steadfastly in
the driveway, not moving a muscle, ears up, staring at us as we
slowly retraced our tracks along the dirt road and back onto the
highway. The Outlaws had to come outside and hold you back
so that you couldn't chase after us. It was so hard to leave
without you. My heart would break into tiny little pieces. You
always had a sadness in your eyes whenever we left. You were
such a precious soul – so damn loyal. You never wanted to
leave my side.

♥♥♥

I guess it's time for me to wrap up stories from our years
at the Abbott house. Before I do, there are just a few more
things I'd like to say…

One Saturday evening, Hubby and I went out for dinner
and later stopped at an electronics store. Hubby had recently
purchased his first computer and wanted to install a new game

called "Myst," an interactive mystery story. We brought it home, flipped on the pc, which was light-years from becoming portable, and began following the trail of clues. It was getting late, so I started doing my nightly chores, one of which was to let you outside for your evening bathroom break before taking you upstairs to bed. After I'd let you out, I laid on the couch, thinking I'd close my eyes for "only a few short minutes." Ha! No such luck. I totally zonked out. It must have been from that belly full of pasta al pomodoro. Hubby was still playing on the computer when I fell asleep and, unbeknownst to comatose me, eventually went upstairs to bed without rousing me. I awoke with a start a few hours later and my mind snapped into rewind. That's when I realized that you were still outside in our backyard. Oh yeah... did I mention that we didn't have a fence? Did I also mention that you weren't on a leash?! I raced to our back door, sure that you'd be nowhere in sight and I'd have to comb the neighborhood. It must have been about one in the morning and all I wanted to do was climb into my nice warm bed. But the thought of you lost or hit by a car sent my heart racing, full speed. I swung open the door and, voila... there you were. Panic attack over. You were patiently lying on our back steps. I can't tell you how overjoyed I was to see you there. Most other dogs would have taken that opportunity to head for the hills of freedom. But not my sweet boy. Nope. Never once did you ever run away from home. You never even ran down the block.

♥♥♥

Diary Entry 7

Dearest Bert,

It's been eleven weeks since you left me. I still miss you terribly. I no longer sob everyday. Instead, the pain has changed from a sharp stab to a dull ache. I still weep, but not as hard as I did at first. My eyes no longer swell up afterwards. I saw one of my bus buddies yesterday. You used to occasionally play with her woofer, Beannie, in Morgan Park. Do you remember? She asked me how you were, and I told her the sad news. Tears welled up in her eyes because she remembered the pain of such a loss all too well. She patted my hand and told me how sorry she was. Last week, a friend of mine sent me a beautiful condolence card. It made me cry so hard. Her words meant so much to me because they came from a place of understanding. She, too, had lost a beloved family member and could relate to the extent of my sorrow. She said that she also kept a journal after her beloved boy passed and cried whenever she wrote in it. She is now able to smile as she reads the passages and assured me that I will be able to do the same one day. I am looking forward to that day.

♥♥♥

The Abbott house had been an extraordinary experience for us all. It was located in a splendid neighborhood, boasting charming stores and restaurants. One of our favorites was Sebastian Joe's, a locally owned and cherished gem. They made the most delicious sorbet to die for. During many summer evenings, we would saddle up you and Ernie then walk over to Joe's for a delectable treat. The shop was nestled amongst several others in Linden Hills. Many other people had the same idea; families with small kids and families with teenagers, couples holding hands, and there were dogs, too, lots and lots of dogs. Hubby would always be the one to go inside and retrieve the summertime goodies while I waited on a bench and held onto you two. You'd usually slump-slide down onto the ground next to me while Ernie begrudgingly sat next to you and whined. Hubby and I would slurp down our cones in front of two transfixed pairs of eyeballs that were hoping to get a bite or two before it was too late. Hard as it was not to devour the whole thing, we never disappointed you.

I loved the way you'd always lay on the ground next to me whenever we were out seeing the sights. You'd casually glance around to see what was going on nearby. Every now and again another dog would catch your eye, or a child would race over and give you a stroke or two. Most of the time you'd patiently wait by my side with your ears up and your eyes bright. Whatever I wanted to do was cool by you, as long as we were together... and I threw in an occasional treat as an added bonus. I miss the feel of you next to me. I miss your beautiful brown eyes glancing at me to see what was next on deck. I miss the adorable way you walked – I guess I'd call it a saunter. You were usually never in much of a hurry, simply happy to be out and about. You were a true expert on the ways and means of how to enjoy life's journey the right way.

❤❤❤

Diary Entry 8

Dearest Bert,

Christmas has come and gone once more. It has now been five and a half months since you left me. Last weekend I went running near Lake Harriet. The water has frozen into ice, and a few people were walking on the lake. There was a guy with his retriever who caught my eye; his dog managed to stay close while zigzagging this way and that, enjoying the beautiful day and its seemingly endless running track. I had to stop for a minute or two when I saw the pair. That dog reminded me so much of you. He was too far away for me to see the details of his face, but I was certain that he was smiling as he loped alongside his guardian, just as you used to do when you were with me. I miss those days of your big, happy smile. Why was it your time to go?

❤❤❤

Do you remember how you used to love to lick Hubby and me all the time? That is one of the things I'll never forget. Non-stop lick, lick, lick. I'm not really sure why you were always out to lick us, but I'd speculate that you were merely trying to express your affection. What seemed like out of nowhere, you developed a funny habit of licking Hubby's legs as soon as he'd finish his daily shower. You tried to do that to me, too, but I gently dissuaded you after a few passes from the pink monster, "No, no, no, my Bert." You easily figured out that your licking obsession just wasn't my thing. Hubby was much easier going. He'd take his shower every morning before work while you were lying on your doggie bed in our bedroom, patiently waiting for him to finish. As soon as you heard him turn off the water, up an' at 'em you'd go, prancing into the bathroom while Hubby was toweling down. That was your cue to take care of his legs. Hubby would let you help out for a minute or two before he'd kiss your snout and relieve you of your post. You'd glumly turn around as if you'd been scolded for not being thorough enough then walk back into the bedroom and plop down on your doggie bed, seemingly exhausted. For as long as I can remember, you and Hubby shared this bonding ritual every single day.

♥♥♥

The Abbott house had a screened front porch, perfect for savoring beautiful summer days, so we purchased some cheapie outdoor wicker furniture not long after we moved in. One evening just after dinner, Hubby and I, along with you and Ernie, were relaxing on our porch, taking pause and listening to the neighborhood. I hadn't been paying attention to anything else and, before I knew it, a salesman had landed right smack dab on our front doorstep. To this day I have absolutely no idea what the poor man was trying to peddle because immediately after he'd rapped his knuckles against the screen door, you bolted upright, raced towards him and began barking

ferociously, all teeth bared. I'd never seen you do that before
and was stunned. And if I think that *I* was startled by your
outburst, the salesman must have been PETRIFIED. I mean,
you weighed almost 100-pounds and were indeed a force to be
reckoned with. Well, I tried so hard not to laugh. I know
that's a terrible reaction, but I couldn't help it. The surprised
fellow jumped backwards in haste, stumbled, and just about
landed on his ass. I apologized profusely and asked if he'd
come back another time, knowing full well that he'd stay as far
away from our house as possible. After he went on his way, I
hugged you and thanked you for protecting your family then
asked you to cool it on the "ferocious lion" bit. You'd made up
your mind somewhere along the line that it was your job to
make certain your family was safe from harm and, by God,
that's exactly what you did. I was never ever afraid to sleep or
walk after dark or do anything, for that matter, as long as you
were by my side. I honestly believe that you would have given
your life to protect me.

♥♥♥

Do you remember how I loved to cook? Me thinks you
loved to be in the kitchen even more than I did. For years and
years you'd sprawl out on your side whenever I'd be in Martha
Stewart mode. You'd lay there and close your eyes while
succulent goodness wafted past your snout. Once in a while,
and much to your great pleasure, a juicy morsel of one variety
or another would plop onto the floor, just waiting for you to
waddle over and gobble it up. Then you'd go back to your
appointed spot of leisure and lay back down. I used to often
make a hearty tomato number that called for a popcorn garnish.
Oh, how you loved it when I'd prepare that soup – it was one
of your favorites. After I'd finish simmering that delicious
concoction, I'd top it off with freshly popped corn and set some
aside for you know who. When Hubby and I were finished
eating dinner, I'd pour a little soup into not one but two dog
bowls, one for you and one for Ernie, then sprinkle it with the

popcorn I'd set aside. I know… seems extravagant, doesn't it?
But, not to me. You were my best friend.

♥♥♥

Well, I guess those are the most prominent memories of
you from our Abbott house. It's time for my reflections to
move on to Morgan Avenue. After a lot of blood, sweat and
tears, oh… and a fair amount of yelling, Hubby and I
completed a full renovation of the Abbott house just a little
more than two years from the date of purchase. It was a huge
accomplishment, to be sure, one that we were both very proud
of. We'd done so much to turn it back into a grand dame, new
kitchen, new bathroom, new landscaping, new everything, but
decided it was time to set aside our attachment and sell it
before we got too settled. Looking toward the future, we set
our sights on locating another distressed damsel in need of
repair, so up went the Abbott house onto the market the very
first weekend in February of 1994, and it sold the same day!
We were astonished and thrilled that everything had gone so
smoothly, it was actually hard to believe. Unbeknownst to us,
we'd stumbled into the real estate game at the start of the
housing bubble when single-family home prices were spiking
like mad. Befuddled were we as we surpassed our initial
asking price by not just leaps, but leaps *and* bounds, having no
idea of the looming trauma and destruction to the real estate
market that would rain down on the American people just
fourteen years later. Sometimes ignorance really does equal
bliss.

So off we headed towards finding another "fixer," fast, and
with it our next adventure. We discovered a hidden gem on
Morgan Avenue, one, which we knew, would sparkle once
more under our care. It was located a mile from our current
location and only one block away from the premier lake in our
great city. Well, that poor thing had been neglected for ages.
It was in the worst shape possible and, in hindsight, knowing
what I know now, I'm stunned that it was never condemned.

We later learned through the neighborhood grapevine that the elderly woman who'd lived there for many years had been an alcoholic and an animal lover to boot, bless her soul. We also discovered that she was not very prudent about cleaning the litter boxes of her ten cats nor letting her numerous canine charges outside for bathroom breaks. Believe me, this explained A LOT. Needless to say, many of the home's once beautiful hardwood floors were saturated with layers of urine and had to be torn up and replaced. The dated living room walls were deep orange and oozed linear, russet colored stains that dripped downward like preserved tears, reeking of the same awful cigarette smoke that infiltrated the remainder of our home. The vintage dining room buffet mirror was so caked with dirt that you couldn't even see your own reflection. The upstairs bathroom (and the only bathroom!) was filthy, forcing us to hire a professional cleaning crew to return it to a somewhat habitable state, which they failed to accomplish, leaving us with no choice but to set up a make-shift restroom in the basement. I could go on and on about the horrible state of that poor, dilapidated girl. I think we were about as crazy as the Outlaws forewarned to have ever embraced that project. In fact, I can't even believe we considered it. The adjective "naïve" is *more than* appropriate. Based solely upon the brashness and stupidity of our youthful years at that time, we fervently succumbed to the location, location, location of that house and kissed a good night's sleep *bye-bye* for months and months to come. When it was all said and done, we were able to bring the Morgan house back to all her shining glory, and then some, but damn! what a struggle it would be.

♥♥♥

Diary Entry 9

Dearest Bert,

It's been ten months now since you left me. So much has happened. I haven't written any passages in my journal for ages. I quit my finance job at Macy's six weeks ago, the one I nabbed after Hubby and I closed the deal and moved into our Morgan Avenue house. I don't really miss it. I guess it was simply time for me to move on. I wish you were here to share these moments of leisure with me. After all, who knows when I'll be back in the rat race again? It's spring now and most of the days have been dewy and warm, ideal for nurturing the restless tulips and daffodils that have remained dormant all winter and are ready to burst into color. I think of you whenever the sunshine streams through the front windows and into the living room and wish we could once again take our morning strolls together, just like we always used to do.

♥♥♥

One of the funniest memories I have from that house is when the police came over. Do you remember that? It was a gorgeous summer day, and I'd just returned from taking you and Ernie for a nice long walk. The three of us were sitting in front of our house, enjoying the warm, mid-afternoon sun. The Morgan house sat high on a hill, providing an incredible overlook above our middle class neighborhood. I was on our front steps sipping a can of pop while you two lazed in the grass nearby when, suddenly, a police car pulled up in front. Two officers nonchalantly got out of their squad and began to approach me. I was taken aback and confused. Don't get me wrong, I was genuinely grateful for their dedicated public service, but I'd never before met a cop who wanted to stop and shoot the bull with me. I figured they must have been looking for *someone* or *something* and chose to speak to the only person who just so happened to be in plain sight. That would be moi. As they moved closer, they took notice of you two, and then one of the officers curtly addressed me, "Ma'am, would you mind taking your dogs inside?"

"Why?" I asked rather snottily. "Is it against the law to hang out with your dogs in your own front yard?" Note to self → The next time a police office approaches, DO NOT, under any circumstances, be a smart ass.

The serious officer seemed unaffected. "Ma'am, just put your dogs inside."

I did as I was told, then they asked if they could step inside my house. Now I was completely floored. What was going on? Why did the cops need to scope my house? By this point I was becoming uneasy, but as soon as they asked me this next question, the whole ordeal became clear... crystal clear.

"Ma'am, did you make a 9-1-1 call about 10 minutes ago?"

"Well.... um... yes," I stammered. "But I didn't mean to. I mean... what I mean is... I tried to call Information at 4-1-1, but I got mixed up, and I guess I called 9-1-1 instead but believe me! as soon as I realized my mistake I hung up." I started getting sweaty. "I am so terribly sorry that I wasted your time, officers. So sorry. Really. I honestly didn't mean to call you."

"Ma'am, we need to investigate *all* 9-1-1 calls. May we take a look around the premises?"

"Sure. Sure," I replied, completely mortified. "Check out anything you want. Anything at all."

The two officers proceeded to survey the main level, and then headed up the stairs to the second. After about ten minutes of investigation, they seemed assured that nothing was amiss. They politely thanked me and told me to be more careful the next time I dialed the phone.

"You bet your sweet ass I'll be more careful," I replied, but only in my head, of course... *this time.*

♥♥♥

Hubby and I completed the major remodeling phase of the Morgan house after an intense ten months. Our kitchen alone had been out of commission for approximately one hundred and forty two days, but who's counting, and boy was I ready to began cooking and baking again. I've always loved to make many of the old standards, like chocolate chip cookies, but I've enjoyed discovering new favorites, too. You and Ernie would lay on the kitchen floor while I whipped up a batch of this or a pan of that. When it came time to bake my concoction du jour, I'd set aside one *whatever* for you and another for Ernie. Oh! How you loved this! A fresh warm treat straight from the oven and into your chops. A couple gulps later and it was long gone, down the hatch. Whenever I was cooking or baking, I'd often pivot from the prep counter to the fridge in order to retrieve an extra ingredient, or else walk over to the cupboard where the pans were stored. You were undoubtedly in my path, forcing me to step over your large girth. It was a little awkward, I'll admit, but I wouldn't have traded it for anything.

♥♥♥

Diary Entry 10

Dearest Bert,

Today is August first. It's now been a whole year since you left me. I'm grateful and relieved that so many days have passed since then. My pain has lessened, but it still haunts me on the inside. I'm now at a place in my life where I can finally smile when I see dogs at play, but I still can't bear to look at your photo, simply because it makes the loss of you seem all the more real. I heard on the news the other day that people in Monrovia, Africa are selling their dogs and cats to slaughterhouses. I was stunned and horrified to my core. Thank the heavens above that I was able to watch over you throughout your entire life and never had to deal with that kind of nightmare.

♥♥♥

Diary Entry 11

Dearest Bert,

It was a tough Labor Day weekend this year. Hubby and I had planned to do all kinds of fun things during our time off, but Ernie became very ill. Your brother was weak and unresponsive. He just laid on his padded bed, eyes staring into the great beyond. He wouldn't even wag his tail when I bent down to kiss the top of his head. We were alarmed, so we took him to the emergency vet. After close examination, the vet determined that Ernie most likely had cancer. It was a very sad day for me. You know how you were my sweetheart and I loved you so, so much, but I did love Ernie, too – just in a different way – and the thought of him dying brings tears to my eyes. He's had such a wonderful life, I know, but still... I imagine that you want your brother by your side again, but I hope he has a little more time down here before he passes over the rainbow. I guess I'm not ready to say good-bye just yet. I mean, after all, Ernie is the second half of the infamous "Bert & Ernie" duo. Once Ernie passes, that chapter of my life will be gone forever. I miss the days when you and Ernie would romp around outside together. You'd always play-fight and tussle, snapping your teeth at each other before rolling around in the dirt. Back then, the thought of you becoming old and slow and tired was so far from my mind. Youth was everywhere; strength abounded. Those days slipped away from me so fast, and now I am once again on the brink of losing another dear one. This has been a painful time for me. I long for the days of playfulness and doggie smiles and joy; the days when I'm happy to live rather than afraid to open the door to my house only to find my best friend lifeless on the dining room floor, or rush my buddy to the ER only to discover that his days are numbered. Bring back the days of gentle breezes on warm summer days and the sound of dog paws digging in the sand as they race along an open beach. Bring back idyllic strolls beside the creek on a bright spring day, the smell of apple blossoms drifting through the air; bring back running on a frozen lake with two dogs in tow, gleefully evading the animal control officer; bring back cool winter evenings at bedtime and finding two dogs contentedly curled up together, covered in warm blankets; bring back crisp autumn days with two dogs in the backyard, lazily passing the day away and half-heartedly chasing the neighborhood squirrels up the elm tree; bring back tails wagging and happy greeting noises after a long, hard day at work; bring back Sunday night dinners where two dogs lounge on the floor after a long, relaxing walk in the leaves. Bring back all those days. Please. Rewind time so that I will know how precious it truly is – so that I will know that I should never have taken one second of it for granted – so that I will know that life is uncertain and nothing lasts. If I knew then what I know now, I wouldn't have to contend with these unhealed wounds.

♥♥♥

Diary Entry 12

Dearest Bert,

It has now been a year and a half since you left me. I still cry now and again whenever I think of you. Your brother is on his last legs. The cancer has a firm grip on him, and it's only a matter of days now before he passes. It's been difficult for me to go through this, but I'm hoping that my sadness over losing Ernie won't be as painful as that which I had to endure when you left. Ernie doesn't seem to get much pleasure from life anymore. Do you remember how both of you loved to go for walks? That was one of your truest joys. I can tell that Ernie's mind wants to relive those days, but his poor, broken body will no longer allow it. He gets a pained look on his face these days as soon as he steps outside and begins to walk around. His spark is almost out now. It will soon be time for life's aches and loss of vitality to come to an end. I can hardly believe that after fourteen years he will no longer be here. It's awful. Hubby has struggled with this dreadful thought just as much as I have, and it's taken a stressful toll on him, indeed. He's been sad and scared and tired for the past four months, ever since Ernie started to deteriorate. I guess, in the end, it will be better for all of us when this is finally over, and then Hubby and I can try to heal.

♥♥♥

Lake Harriet was so pretty in the winter, especially after a thick blanket of luscious snow. Practically everybody in our neighborhood would break out their cross-country skis and zip around the three-mile rim of the lake. Big snows and cross-country skiing make a delightful combination. One evening, I talked Hubby into bringing you and Ernie along. Our Morgan house was only a block and a half away, making it a snap to haul our gear down to what once had been a beach just a few short months ago. The big bright moon soared above piles of freshly fallen, silky powder. It wasn't really all that cold, and the wind was silent and still. We grabbed our ski gear and made sure you and Ernie were ready, too. Hubby and I began to glide around the lake while both of you ran behind, sans leash. Do you remember Ernie that night? What a blast he had! He ran like fury... beside us, behind us, in front of us. You name it. He ran and ran and ran. It was more difficult for you to run in the snow because you just weren't built like Mr. Ernie, a lean, mean running machine; you were stuck with a lot more bulk to carry around. And unlike Ernie's smooth, fur-free paws, yours were covered in gobs of hair that unfailingly manufactured mini snowballs; my poor boy got socked with freak-of-nature snowball paws! Every now and again, you'd lag behind your pack so that you could gnaw at the pesky icicles that gathered in-between your toes, and then off you'd sprint to catch up with us. Hubby would get mad whenever you attempted to stay abreast, which I found utterly hilarious. You'd repeatedly lumber onto the backs of our skis, causing us to trip, and Hubby would yell, "Bert! Would you please stop that!" I'd try not to laugh. It never really bothered me; it wasn't your fault, you just didn't want to get left behind. Our snowy adventure lasted about forty-five minutes. I enjoyed it immensely, all of it; the crispness of the winter air that kissed my cheeks; the foreboding, dark beauty of the icy lake; the mesmerizing glow of white. You and Ernie both loved it, too. After we completed our loop, Hubby and I removed our skis and headed up the small hill that led us home. We toweled off the two of you, flanks and feet soaked from play, before shuttling you into the comfy, warm house where soft beds and blankets awaited. Ahhhh…. We all slept so well on those evenings.

♥♥♥

Diary Entry 13

Dearest Bert,

Sweet little Ernie died today. His spark was completely gone; the cancer had finally beat him down and life was no longer a joy, only pain remained. Hubby and I took him to the vet one last time. On the way over, we stopped at Bone Adventure and bought him one of his favorite snacks. He ate a little at first but then turned away. I could tell that he was having a difficult time remaining here on this earth. Hubby carried Ernie inside when we arrived at the vet's office. Witnessing the life of a dear friend drift past in the blink of an eye is unspeakably horrible and surreal at the same time. It was one of the worst experiences of my life. Before we'd left the house, I remembered to slip your collar into my coat pocket. I wanted to be extra sure that the collars of two best friends were united at the moment of Ernie's passing so that he would be sure to find you. I know that you have been missing him. He was such a sweet boy with a good heart. I loved Ernie and feel sad that he no longer runs like the wind through the trees.

♥♥♥

When you were about eight years old, I decided to take you and Ernie running with me on wintry Sunday afternoons. Although both of you were still vibrant, it was becoming apparent that you were beginning to slow just a little. I plotted a 2-mile route near our Morgan house that took us through the neighborhood and over to Minnehaha Creek, then back again. It was such a blast because I could unleash you once we got to the creek path to frolic in the snow just as though you were puppies again. It was wonderful to see you so joyful out in the fresh air instead of cooped up for months 'til summer came back around. So there we were each Sunday, the three of us running together, well… sort of together, in the frosty air. Once back home, we'd race up the concrete steps that led to the front porch, and I'd grab a towel from a basket that we kept beside the wicker chair then dry off your damp bodies, and then your faces and feetsies before letting you inside. You loved it best when I'd wipe the excess moisture from your face with a soft towel. Ernie especially loved it. I honestly believe he thought I was giving him gentle cotton kisses on his cheeks and forehead. After that, we'd barrel into the nice warm, cozy house and you both would make a beeline, in tandem, for the water bowl. Gulp, gulp, gulp… the cool water tasted so refreshing after a long run. The two of you would then walk side by side into the living room and lay down on the rug while Hubby and I watched our favorite Sunday night TV shows and ate dinner. The three of us did "The Dog Walk" run for several more seasons, until one day, a day that seemed to come out of nowhere, your body stubbornly insisted that it was much too tired for such shenanigans, bookmarking the end of one more chapter in your life.

♥♥♥

We all loved going to the park and had many lovelies from which to choose. Whenever we'd arrive at the day's chosen rec area, at least one dog, or sometimes even several, would be hurtling themselves at each other and leaping about. The other puppy parents would usually let their dogs play with the two of you, and so would begin our ritual… "Sit Boys" and you'd both sit down. I'd then remove your leashes. "Stay Boys"… and I'd insist that you stayed put for a second or maybe even two, at least long enough to give the "appearance" that you were actually listening to me. "Okay!" I'd shout, and that lone magic word would send the two of you flying off to a destination unknown = nowhere in particular. I highly doubt either of you had the slightest idea where you were headed.

Your bro always had a few tricks up his sleeve. If there weren't any other dogs around, then Ernie would snap his teeth at you. Do you remember that? He'd try to tease you into chasing him, and you fell for it… every single time. But if there were any other four-legged loiterers in the park, then Ernie would find a way to entice them into his web. That Ernie was such a clever boy. He was the master of trickery and could scam any dog into the Chase Game. I have no earthly idea how he was able to hold them all like putty in the palm of his paw, but he never failed. It was like watching a professional con artist in Vegas. Once he got them sucked in using his own special brand of hypnotics, the chase would begin. Of course, none of the other dogs could catch Ernie, ever. Not even close. Ernie truly loved being the mob boss. If ever there were moments of glory for that dog, those were undoubtedly it. Most of Ernie's life off the playing field was spent as an extremely submissive dog, especially in times of conflict. I'm

talkin' rolling onto his back at the slightest lip curl from a
burlier brute. But on the playing field of the Chase Game?
Well, that was a *whole* different ballgame. Ernie was the
undisputed king. He could fly through grass like he was a half-
breed cheetah. Sure, a few of the bigger, stronger dogs were
players, and they'd get close, but never quite close enough.
They didn't have nothin' on Ernie and the boy knew it. Not
only did he know it, but he relished every single second. If he
could have shouted "Na-na-Na-na-Na!" at the top of his lungs,
he would have. To look at Ernie when he was lounging on the
ground, you would've never guessed he could break the sound
barrier. He was a lean 60 pounds, not at all tall and rather on
the stocky side. Let's just say he didn't even come close to
having the body of a greyhound. But man, the boy could run.
You, on the other hand, my sweet, lanky Bert, were a big
mush-ball slowpoke. The only time you ever came close to
catching Ernie was when you were a really young boy, but
your ability to compete didn't last long. The majority of your
mid-life years were spent bringing up the rear of the pack,
well… sort of. You always had a certain bewildered look on
your face, as though you were running with the young guns for
no other reason than because *they* were running.   You'd
quickly tire of such frivolity and ease into a complete stop
while barking like a jealous cheerleader. It was as if you were
telling everybody to "knock it off!" Around and around Ernie
would take the other woofers. One lap, two laps, three laps,
four. The group would finally disband for reasons unknown,
and then the other puppy parents would reel in their pooches.
Homeward bound, we would complete the circle we'd begun
… happy smiles on beautiful faces.

❤❤❤

Do you remember how Ernie loved it when you'd lick his
ears? I'm not sure how that all got started, I think the two of
you just got bored sometimes. Ernie would flop down next to
you and roll onto his side to strategically position his head "just

right" in order for you to bend your neck and lick his ears for minutes upon minutes. It was so soothing to Ernie. He was in heaven. He'd lay there with his eyes half closed and the most contented look on his face. It was as if he were enjoying a luxurious spa treatment. Most of the time you seemed to be fine with your role as Ernie's caretaker and oblige him whenever he begged for favors. In this particular case, you'd lick his ears for a short while, and then stop suddenly, as if disgusted. With his bright eyes Ernie would beg you to continue… please, please, please continue… won't you please continue… please? You'd begrudgingly begin again until you just couldn't take it any longer and look up at me with those big, sorrowful eyes that pleaded for help. Enough was enough. You'd stand up and move a mere few feet away from your bro then flop back down. Ernie was on his own! For a while, anyway, until he'd beg you for something else.

♥♥♥

One of my most favorite memories of you was when you'd lay on the carpeted landing at the Morgan House. Our main set of stairs, which led from the first level to the second, had one ninety degree turn in the middle which required a landing, the perfect place for you to rest and contemplate your next covert Snausage drawer operation. Your mission was to successfully infiltrate our kitchen and retrieve as many snacks as possible before you-know-me caught you-know-you red handed. Not only was it an exceptionally soft and cozy spot for reflection, but it also served as a strategic vantage point from which to attack any unsuspecting intruder who just might happen to make the fatal mistake of sneaking through our front door. You were our appointed guard dog, 24/7, at least that's how you saw it. You'd always make me smile whenever I happened to be passing your favorite outpost. Your eyes would usually be closed, sometimes meditatively so, with your big pink tongue flopping from the side of your mouth, practically touching the carpet. I'd stop to kiss your cheek and hug you, or ruffle your fur with little love taps. Do you remember?

♥♥♥

You were the most gorgeous boy, and I'm not just saying that because I loved you so damn much. You only had one teensy weensy annoying physical trait, and that was the length of your fur. It was beautiful, to be sure, an orange-brownish color, but so very l-o-n-g, so very, very l-o-n-g. And I just happen to be so very l-a-z-y, so very, very l-a-z-y when it came to picking up a comb and using it. Not the best combo. I never managed it like I should have, so your fur would predictably rebel at my lack of attentiveness, becoming matted in no time flat. Your disheveled state of physical existence never seemed to bother my little hippie boy much, and it usually didn't bother me either, *except* when you had to go to the groomer. Ugggghhhh. I hated taking you to the dreaded groomer. Throughout all those years, I never learned my lesson to appropriately tend to your locks and would be forced to send you off to Bone Adventure in a terrible matted mess. They would have to spend four plus hours on your beauty treatment, trying to remove those dastardly mats. My poor punkin' would shake with fear every time we entered the premises. I was always so relieved when I received the call informing me that you were a clean, brand new boy and ready to go home, festooned with a swanky neck bandana and all. The employees would tell me what a sweet boy you were and how patient you'd been throughout the hellish ordeal, licking your prison guards the entire time. Yes, that's how you were, a gigantic heart of gold. I can still remember how you'd always lick my hands or arms for no other reason than just because they were near. You'd run your soft tongue tenderly along the side of my arm, your gentle licks long and slow, never rushed. I love you so much, Bert and still miss you terribly. It has been almost two years since you left me.

If any dog was obsessed with food, it was definitely you, without question. The following list is a physical representation of love as told through the eyes of the best damn dog on the planet:

#1 BFF – Female Edition
#2 BFF – Male Edition
#3 Food
#4 Walks
#5 Ernie
#6 Brethren Kitty Folk

Hard as I tried to maintain your proper weight, I'd inevitably receive an annual scolding from our family vet. "He needs to get leaner," she'd advise. In all honesty, I could never understand why you weren't more svelte. After all, I only fed you twice a day. Okay, so maybe daily snacks were involved, but they were infinitesimal. Itty bitty things they were. Anyway, I really did try my darndest to keep you in the best shape possible by feeding you nutritious food and giving you daily exercise, but you were a natural born gourmand and there wasn't much I could do about it. When you were just a young pup, you'd sit right next to Hubby and I while we were enjoying dinner and stare right at us, your hungry laser beams tracking the fork from our plates to our lips and then back again. A few minutes later, drool would slowly begin to pool in both corners of your mouth, eventually gathering to such abundance that gravity would give way and all the excess would slither down onto the carpet. This drove me nuts, so I decided early on that it was just fine and dandy for you and Ernie to sit with us during dinner, but you would no longer be allowed to watch and drool. I developed a mealtime regimen whereby I trained both of you to lay next to us on the floor, eyes averted, while Hubby and I ate our meals in saliva-free peace. Afterwards, the two of you would get your well-earned morsels from the feast. This seemed to do the trick. I never ceased to be amazed by your uncanny ability to listen for the telltale sounds of a completed meal while looking in the opposite direction. You always, always knew… one minute you were laying beside me in mock repose, pretending not to care about baked lasagna, then the next minute you'd snap to attention faster than the queen's guard whenever I'd rise from my seated position. The clinking of the dinner plates was your cue to spring up, then off we'd go into the kitchen. I'd place equal helpings into each of your food bowls. Well okay, sometimes I *might have* given you a little extra, but you did weigh thirty pounds more than Ernie. Both of you could hardly stand the wait, and you'd begin to prance ... one foot forward, one foot back, prancing to and fro, side to side. And then I'd stand back and let you have at it. Gone within sixty seconds. After you'd inhaled it, I'd always ask, "Now, did you ever taste any of that???" You'd innocently look up at me and lick your lips. I guess that was my answer.

♥♥♥

Final Diary Entry

Dearest Bert-

It has been two years now since you left me. I bought a frame for your photo today. I'm not sure if I'll ever be able to use it. The way you died is too hard for me to think about. Do you remember how hot it was that August? I had such a hard time keeping the house cool enough for you. You'd never liked hot weather much, but that summer was harder on you than ever before. You'd pant and pace a lot. Something wasn't adding up – something was wrong. I placed a bed sheet on top of the couch for you to lie upon and cranked the air conditioner each morning before I left for work. I hired a dog walker to check on you mid-afternoon a few times a week. She was kind and would try to muster you outside for a short walk, but would later report that most days you never wanted to leave the couch. I guess I should have listened better to what you were trying to tell me, but I was still stuck in the past, stuck back all those years ago when walks were on your short list. I told myself that it was good for you to get some fresh air until I could return home later in the evening. It was just the two of us by that time, me and you. Hubby and I didn't make it. Who knows what went wrong. I guess it doesn't really matter now anyway. Hubby was now The Ex and took care of Ernie while I had you. You'd always been my favorite boy after all, even though I sometimes felt guilty about admitting it. Paying the bills and taking care of a house solo for the first time in my life was scary as hell. I became overwhelmed and started drinking wine each evening after work, lots and lots of it. It made me tired most of the time. Not the kind of tired one feels from running here and there and everywhere, but the kind of worn-out-from-life tired. I became permanently cranky. Through it all I still had you, and I needed you to be there for me. Maybe that's why I ignored the warning signs. Maybe I wasn't strong enough to realize what was coming. Do you remember that night before you died? The evening air was sweltering, and I was sick of listening to that damn air conditioner of ours, so I opened the windows, exposing the screen and all the outside noise along with it. Low and behold a few of the neighbor cats were fighting in the driveway near our bedroom. They were fire engine loud and woke me up around 2:00 in the morning. I had a heck of a time getting back to sleep. When the alarm rang at 5:30 the next morning I was feisty as all get out from lack of slumber. I glanced over at you lying on your doggie bed near the wall. You weren't stirring much. I sat up and rubbed my face but the pounding in my head wouldn't go away. "C'mon Bert. C'mon. We've got to get moving. Get up now so that we can get our walk in before work." You didn't look like you wanted to go on no walk, no way. You didn't look like you wanted to go anywhere. But I wasn't paying much attention because my head was pounding. I'd had too much wine the night before and not nearly enough sleep. I went into the bathroom and brushed my teeth then put on the nearest

*pair of shorts and a tank top. Typically by this point you'd
have sauntered through the kitchen and over to the side door,
the one we always used to go outside. But that morning you
were lying on your bed, semi-lifeless. I was in a hurry now,
"C'mon Bert! We've got to go! You know I have to be to work
soon!" You slowly rose and did your best to comply. Out the
door we went and took off on our usual 20-minute route. In the
year and a half since we'd lived at the Harriet house, you'd
slowly been losing ground. In the beginning we'd been able to
cover a fair amount of real estate in that time and clipped right
along, but by now your saunter had set itself to turtle pace and
you could only walk a few blocks, just enough time to sniff a
few fire hydrants and decode the messages left by the other
woofers before turning around and urging me back home.*

*It was a Thursday, I'll never forget that it was a Thursday.
I'd taken the next day off from work so that I could enjoy a
long weekend with you. Before leaving that morning, I gave
you my usual hug and kiss, turned on the air and promised you
we'd take a fun, relaxing walk on Friday. Work was hard
during that period of time. Not taxing my brain hard, but just
boring hard, sick-of-office-politics hard, I-hate-my-boss hard.
Plus I was always exhausted from all the damn wine I was now
consuming; forget about liquid lunch, how about liquid dinner
nearly every night of the week. It took a lot less time to
prepare and there was only one choice to make, would it be red
this evening or white? I managed to zombie through that
Thursday and successfully completed all my work assignments,
relieved to be in the car with The Boyfriend after the five
o'clock bell rang, heading back home to you. Ya ba da ba -
Doooo!! I was edgy after The Boyfriend dropped me off.
There I stood outside my side entrance, fumbling through my
purse, trying to find my house keys. I was thinking of stupid
stuff, like work and whether or not The Boyfriend was going to
call me on Saturday. When I opened the door and entered, you
didn't trot over to greet me. That was weird. In all the years
we'd been together, you'd never missed a single day. I
absentmindedly set my purse down and began to take off my*

shoes. "Bert! Bert!" I called, thinking you were fast asleep on the couch and couldn't hear me over the buzz of the air conditioner. As soon as I stepped farther into the kitchen I could better see through the entry into my dining room. "Oh my God, Bert? Bert?!" And there you were, lying lifeless in my dining room, your eyes still open. I don't really want to talk about this part – it's really still too painful, even after all this time. I was simply devastated and not handling the situation well at all. After I thought I'd composed myself, I rang The Boyfriend and lost it again, sobbing uncontrollably. Through my tears, I asked if he'd drive back to my house and help me rush you to my family vet. He sped back and ran inside the house, only to find me in a pool of anguish down on the floor next to you. I got myself together just enough to help him carry you to the car, and then off we went. The staff at the vet's office was horrible, beyond horrible really, looking at me as though I were crazy for bringing my dead dog into their office. I frantically begged them, "Please, please, can't you just see if there's any heart beat at all?!" The vet tech on duty hesitated before begrudgingly complying. He took your vacant, 100-pound body from us then headed into an exam room and thumped you down onto the steel table, as if you weren't due any respect. He was shaking his head, trying to find polite words, but I knew he just wanted to tell me I was a nut job. After a minute or so, he curtly explained that there was nothing he could do. "He's dead," he stated frankly. I was so distraught that I wasn't capable of telling him to blaze off and thanks for being such a jerk, by the way. I just shut down right then and there, resigning myself to the fact that you weren't breathing and you hadn't done so in the twenty minutes since I found you unresponsive. That was it. You were gone, never to return. My life would forever be emptier from that point forward.

To this day I still don't know what caused your death. Was it a heart attack? The heat? Or was it all those injections the vet insisted you needed just a week before? "Bert needs a distemper shot and is overdue for the rabies one as well. You may as well give him a Lyme disease preventative as long as you're here." Reminding my vet that you were an elderly twelve years old by that point, I questioned whether all these treatments were really necessary. She assured me they were. Now I'm not so sure.

All my tears, my anguish, my sorrow can't bring you back. Nothing can. The only things I have left now are these memories I've written down and a lock of your golden hair to place in my diary. You were one of the best dogs there ever was my sweet Bert. Were you lucky that I came along that day at the Animal Humane Society and adopted you? Sure. I'll admit it, sure you were. But I was, by far, the luckiest one of all.

♥♥♥
♥♥♥
♥♥♥

A Personal Note from the Author:

Hi! A huge thanks to you for taking the time to read Letters to Bert. If you enjoyed my story, I'd be thrilled to receive a quick review from you on Amazon. I never take a single word of praise for granted, your comments mean that much to me.

Wishing you many more wonderful adventures with your own four-legged hero. Dogs paint our world in beautiful colors, and it would sure be a boring place here without them to brighten our days.

X & O………….Tera